T0275341

THE OFFICIAL WORKBOOK
MINECRAFT
GRADE 3

Written by Russell Ginns

Illustrations by Antonio Vecchione

WELCOME TO
A LEARNING ADVENTURE!

This workbook lets kids practice essential skills while taking a journey through the world of Minecraft. Practice multiplication while exploring a cave and storytelling while battling a dragon! There are dozens of activities filled with reading, math, and critical-thinking skills, all set among the biomes, mobs, and loot of your child's favorite game.

Special Minecraft Missions at the end of each lesson also send readers on learning challenges inside and outside the book!

Here are some tips to make the most of this workbook:

- Make sure your child has a quiet, comfortable place to work.

- Give your child a variety of pencils, crayons, and any other items they may need to write answers, draw pictures, or set up games.

- Read the directions with your child. There's a lot of information and adventures packed into each chapter! You can help tell the stories and point out the basic tasks that need to be done.

- Spend extra time on any section that your child finds difficult.

- Enjoy the fun Minecraft facts and jokes with your child. This is your chance to learn more about a game that interests them!

Grab a pen or pencil and get ready to have fun as you learn with Minecraft!

WILD IN THE JUNGLE

You've arrived in the jungle. There are useful things to collect...and things to watch out for, too.

In this adventure, you will...

Gather wood.

Discover animals.

Avoid booby traps.

Explore a temple.

Let's get started!

Gather wood by punching trees.

Circle all the **nouns** (words that are people, places, or things).

house

bird

sing

wet

large

tree

beach

raced

loud

push

tiger

shovel

MINECRAFT FACT: Dark oak trees are some of the tallest in the world of Minecraft.

Draw a line between pairs of sticks to make **nouns**. Write each full word in the spaces to the right.

/ fa   / met   _____

/ fie   / rm   _____

/ fi   / ld   _____

/ hel   / sh   _____

/ t   / ood   _____

/ vin   / ower   _____

/ f   / e   _____

/ lis   / ord   _____

/ sw   / t   _____

There are pandas, parrots, and many other things in the jungle. Keep track of them as you explore.

Sort the words from the list below into categories by writing them in the correct boxes. Cross each word out as you categorize it. The leftover words will give you a hint as to what comes next.

tree	pig	Enderman	shirt	bamboo	something
cow	zombie	special	boots	is	skeleton
cocoa	hidden	ocelot	hat	here	frog
sheep	creeper	leggings	melon	grass	chicken

Plants

_____

_____ _____

_____ _____

MINECRAFT FACT: Pandas live in the jungle because it is the only place that has bamboo, which they love to snack on.

Friendly Mobs

_____   _____

_____   _____

Clothes

_____   _____

_____   _____

Hostile Mobs

_____   _____

_____   _____

— — — — — — — — —   — — — — — —

— — — — — — — — — —

You find a temple. Watch out for any hidden dangers as you explore inside.

Find a path from **START** to **END** without triggering any tripwires.

As you move along the path, you will travel over many tripwires. You can disable them and pass safely only if the line connects two **pronouns** (words such as **I**, **you**, **we**, **he**, **she**, **it**, or **they**).

If you see a line that does not connect two pronouns—watch out! Don't cross, or it will send arrows at you, and you'll have to start over.

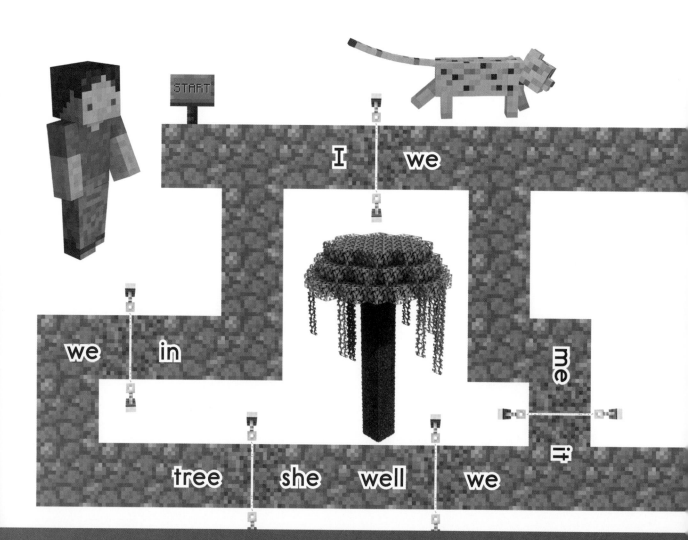

MINECRAFT FACT: Jungle temples have booby traps that fire arrows.

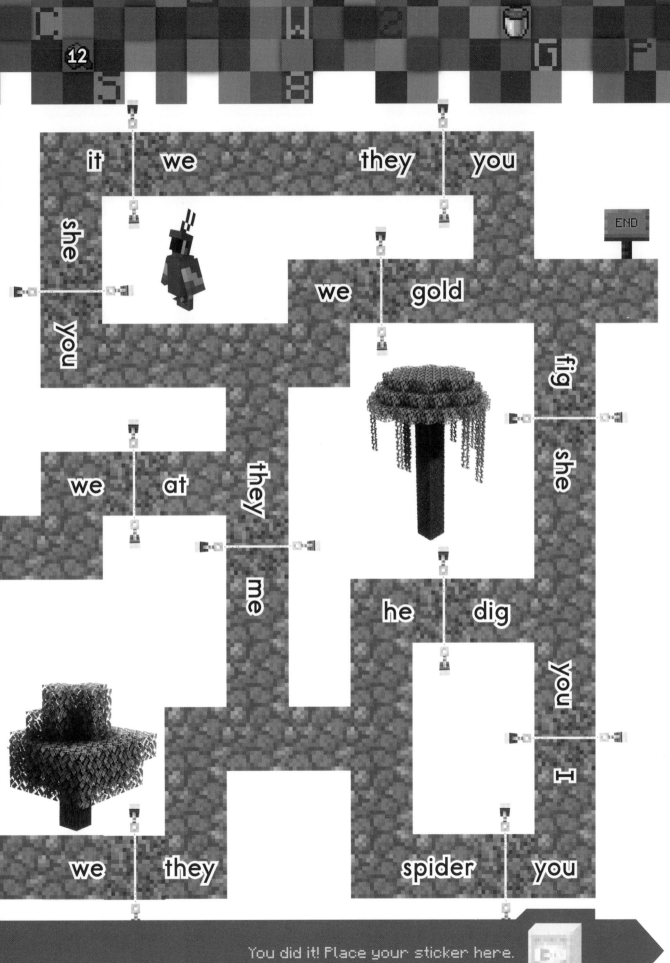

it   we   they   you

she

END

you

we   gold

fig

she

we   at   they   me

he   dig

you

I

we   they   spider   you

You did it! Place your sticker here.

Find the exit to the temple to get a better view of your surroundings.

Find a path from **START** to **END**. You can only go sideways or up, never down. And you can only pass through **plural** words.

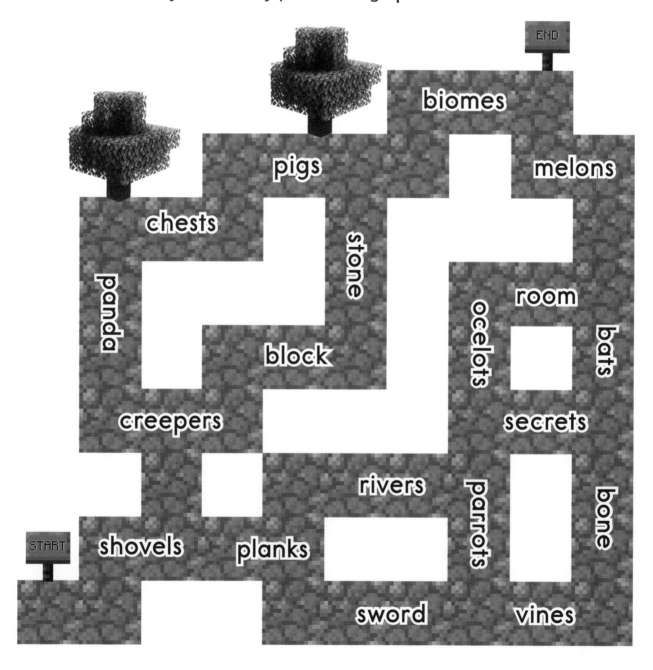

What can't be pushed around in the jungle?   A tem-pull!

Cross out every **plural** word. Then write all the remaining words in the spaces at the bottom to find out what you see after you climb the temple.

hills mobs there

is a

ferns trees

logs

mountain far

adventures

huts in

the clouds nests

bees distance

_ _ _ _ _   _ _   _

_ _ _ _ _ _ _ _   _ _ _

_ _   _ _ _   _ _ _ _ _ _ _ _

You did it! Place your sticker here.

MINECRAFT MISSION

From the top of the temple, you can see a faraway mountain. Before you head there, take a break and try this special challenge.

This mission sends you *outside* of this book!

Your task is to explore the different regions of your house in search of things that fit these rules:

- Find two things with names that contain at least three of the same letters

- Find something with a name that contains three different **vowels**

- Find two different things that **rhyme**

- Find a book with a front cover that does *not* contain the letter **s**

Write down the things you find. When you are done, find the correct sticker and place it in the lower corner. You've completed your first mission!

_____   _____

_____   _____

_____   _____

MINECRAFT EXPLORE

Great job! You earned a badge! Place your sticker here.

BUILD

MOUNTAIN HIDEAWAY

High on a mountain is a great place to build a new home.

In this adventure, you will...

Climb a mountain.

Fight skeletons.

Gather stone.

Build a home.

Let's get started!

Navigate the uneven terrain of the mountain.

Solve these **addition** problems to climb the mountain.

$$200 + 12 = \rule{3cm}{0.4pt}$$

$$382 + 500 = \rule{3cm}{0.4pt}$$

$$60 + 23 = \rule{3cm}{0.4pt}$$

$$74 + 17 = \rule{3cm}{0.4pt}$$

$$448 + 22 = \rule{3cm}{0.4pt}$$

$$100 + 11 = \rule{3cm}{0.4pt}$$

$$231 + 22 = \rule{3cm}{0.4pt}$$

$$17 + 10 = \rule{3cm}{0.4pt}$$

$$28 + 2 = \rule{3cm}{0.4pt}$$

MINECRAFT FACT: Players can only jump about one block up, so stacking blocks helps reach higher areas.

Solve these **subtraction** problems to climb down the mountain.

200 - 12 = _____

500 - 382 = _____

100 - 11 = _____

399 - 89 = _____

171 - 12 = _____

68 - 12 = _____

87 - 17 = _____

16 - 15 = _____

28 - 2 = _____

As the sun sets, you hear loud rattling sounds.
Skeletons have found you!

Solve these **addition** problems to fire arrows at them.

$31 + 4 + 4 =$ _____

$12 + 3 + 3 =$ _____

$1 + 14 + 9 =$ _____

$8 + 2 + 32 =$ _____

$55 + 2 + 8 =$ _____ $62 + 5 + 7 =$ _____

$48 + 6 + 5 =$ _____ $5 + 9 + 37 =$ _____

$89 + 2 + 4 =$ _____ $16 + 4 + 5 =$ _____

$6 + 1 + 72 =$ _____ $7 + 2 + 41 =$ _____

MINECRAFT FACT: There are different variations of skeletons in Minecraft. All of them are hostile mobs.

Solve these **subtraction** problems to dodge the skeletons' arrows.

87 - 1 - 5 = ___

12 - 2 - 8 = ___

67 - 2 - 7 = ___

55 - 11 - 4 = ___

49 - 18 - 2 = ___   49 - 36 - 1 = ___

87 - 65 - 43 = ___   78 - 23 - 5 = ___

29 - 14 - 2 = ___   99 - 23 - 12 = ___

34 - 12 - 9 = ___   85 - 43 - 38 = ___

You did it! Place your sticker here.

You can find a lot of stone in the mountains. Collect some so you can build a home at a clearing.

Write the symbol for **addition (+)** or **subtraction (−)** in the boxes to finish each equation.

15 ☐ 25 = 40   74 ☐ 18 = 92

19 ☐ 10 = 9   84 ☐ 38 = 122

10 ☐ 66 = 76   47 ☐ 7 = 40

88 ☐ 17 = 71   72 ☐ 11 = 83

24 ☐ 14 = 10   44 ☐ 54 = 98

63 ☐ 19 = 44   89 ☐ 19 = 70

1 ☐ 1 = 0   56 ☐ 16 = 40

MINECRAFT FACT: Exposed ores are often hiding beneath snow and ice.

300 ☐ 300 = 0

282 ☐ 77 = 359

176 ☐ 22 = 154

298 ☐ 321 = 619

201 ☐ 400 = 601

444 ☐ 333 = 777

821 ☐ 410 = 411

819 ☐ 19 = 838

136 ☐ 258 = 394

You've gathered stone, and you've made a clearing.
It's a great place to build a mountain hideaway.

Write a number in each empty box. The numbers in every column, row, and diagonal must add up to the number in the roof above it. The first one has been done for you.

15

8	3	4
1	5	9
6	7	2

21

12	3	
	7	
6	11	

What did the crafter say when you gave them some wood blocks? Planks a lot.

34

16			13
		10	
9	7		12
	14		1

38

5			2
		7	13
	12	11	
17	3		

You did it! Place your sticker here.

MINECRAFT MISSION

You've built a cozy new home in the mountains. Now that you're safe, take this challenge.

This mission sends you on a search *inside* this book.

There are six pages with **skeletons** () hidden at the top. Find them and write the numbers from each skeleton in the spaces below.

_____   _____   _____

_____   _____   _____

Now use those numbers to complete this magic square!

6	3		
9		5	
	2	11	14
	13	8	1

MINECRAFT BUILD

Great job! You earned a badge! Place your sticker here.

22

HOST WITH THE MOST

Friends are coming over for a party. When they arrive, they will be expecting full hospitality.

In this adventure, you will...

Collect milk.

Harvest wheat.

Gather eggs and sugar cane.

Craft a cake.

Let's get started!

Grab a bucket. It's time to collect milk!

Follow the paths that have only **verbs** (words that are actions) to reach each cow.

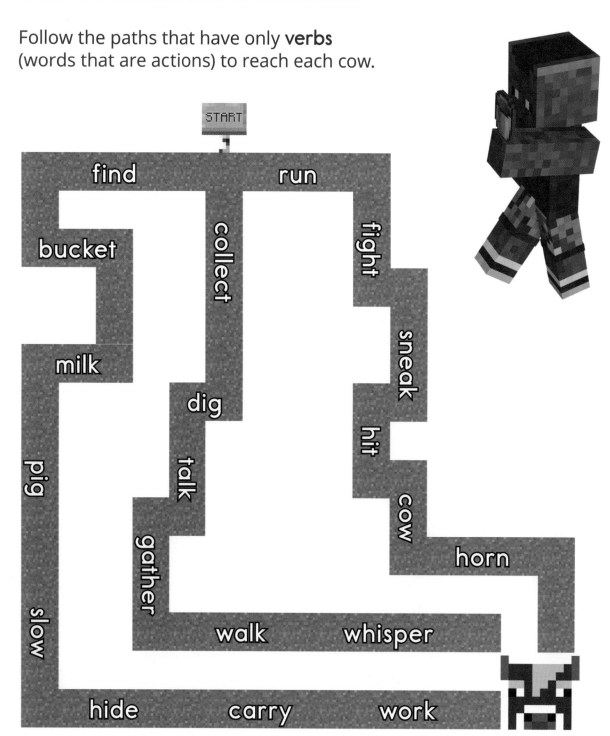

START

find   run

bucket   collect   fight

milk   sneak

dig   hit

pig   talk   cow

gather   horn

slow   walk   whisper

hide   carry   work

MINECRAFT FACT: In the game, using a bucket on a cow will give you milk.

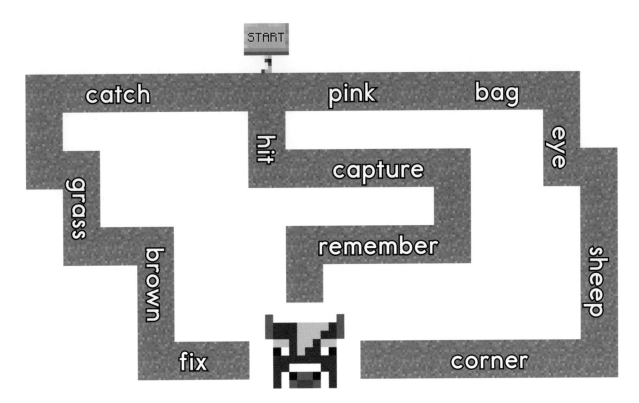

START

catch · pink · bag · eye · hit · capture · grass · remember · sheep · brown · fix · corner

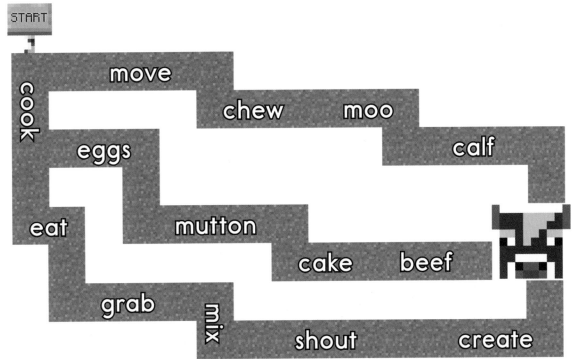

START

move · cook · chew · moo · eggs · calf · eat · mutton · cake · beef · grab · mix · shout · create

Walk into the field and harvest wheat to bring home.

Walk, **harvest**, and **bring** are all **verbs**. Now find more verbs in the word search on page 27. Words go up, down, across, backward, and diagonally.

When you're done, write the leftover letters in the spaces below. They will tell you something about your visitors.

Find these words:					
build	cover	gather	keep	run	tell
climb	dig	give	pull	see	try
collect	explain	hear	punch	tap	win

— — — —   — — —

— — — — — !

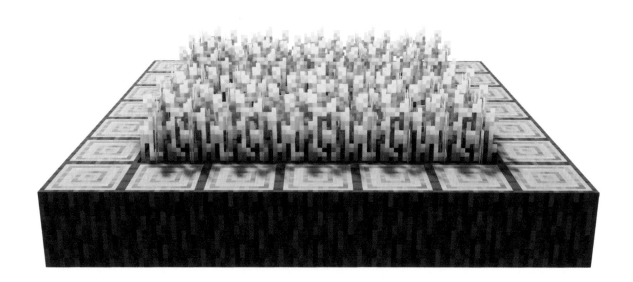

MINECRAFT FACT: Wheat seeds are common and can be collected while breaking tall grass.

T	T	C	E	L	L	O	C
B	H	E	Y	L	R	E	O
U	D	I	G	U	U	X	V
I	K	E	E	P	N	P	E
L	A	V	R	U	E	L	R
D	I	W	I	N	P	A	T
G	H	U	N	C	E	I	E
T	R	Y	G	H	R	N	L
R	E	H	T	A	G	Y	L
C	L	I	M	B	S	E	E

You did it! Place your sticker here.

Find more food. Look for sugar cane and eggs. Then run home and cook for your friends.

Underline the **verbs** in each sentence. The first one has been done for you.

The adventurer <u>harvests</u> sugar cane.

They gaze over the land.

They hear the sound of water.

They see something that moves back and forth.

A chicken runs along the river.

They catch it and collect eggs!

MINECRAFT FACT: Sugar can be crafted from sugar cane.

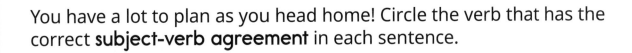

You have a lot to plan as you head home! Circle the verb that has the correct **subject-verb agreement** in each sentence.

My friends is are coming soon.

They love loves to eat.

I will make made them a delicious meal.

Mixes Mixing eggs, sugar, milk,

and wheat is are messy.

When I am is done, we will are eat.

The cake look looks beautiful.

Craft a cake, put it all together...and throw a party!

Read each sentence. Then circle **past**, **present**, or **future** to show when it is happening.

I collected all the things I needed.

past present future

Eggs and sugar are good for baking.

past present future

My friends are on their way.

past present future

I will bake them a cake.

past present future

The cake looks yummy.

past present future

Why did the adventurer fall asleep at the party? They used a NAP-kin!

I am putting up colorful decorations.

past present future

We played games at the party.

past present future

Everyone had a good time.

past present future

Now my home is a mess.

past present future

I forgot to invite my friend the golem.

past present future

It will enjoy the next party.

past present future

I will make more cakes next time!

past present future

You did it! Place your sticker here.

MINECRAFT MISSION

You've decorated your home for your Minecraft party. Now decorate your room in real life.

This mission sends you *outside* of this book! Decorate your room using some words from this adventure.

You'll need:

- Crayons
- Paper
- Pencils
- Scissors
- Tape

Make a door hanger! Make some labels to put on some things you own. Make a to-do list or a poster about your favorite game.

Here's where the challenge comes in: Everything you make must contain at least one verb. Also, you are not allowed to repeat a verb.

Does this **seem** fun? **Are** you ready to **start**? Go!

MINECRAFT
BAKE

Great job! You earned a badge! Place your sticker here.

GO THROUGH A CAVE

Not far from your mountain hideaway, you spot a cave.

In this adventure, you will...

Enter a mineshaft.

Open chests.

Craft a minecart.

Repair rails.

Let's get started!

You follow a wooden path that leads into a mineshaft.

Solve these **multiplication** problems to light the path.

$7 \times 1 = \underline{\quad}$ $9 \times 3 = \underline{\quad}$

$10 \times 1 = \underline{\quad}$ $12 \times 1 = \underline{\quad}$

$6 \times 2 = \underline{\quad}$ $20 \times 2 = \underline{\quad}$

$9 \times 2 = \underline{\quad}$ $11 \times 3 = \underline{\quad}$

$8 \times 2 = \underline{\quad}$

$4 \times 3 = $

MINECRAFT FACT: Mineshafts are a series of tunnels that may spawn under your world. They connect many caves and other underground areas.

Find a path from **START** to **END**. You can only pass through an opening if the equation is correct.

As you explore, you come across many chests.

Solve these **multiplication** problems to see what's inside.

$4 \times 4 =$ _____

$12 \times 5 =$ _____

$10 \times 4 =$ _____

$11 \times 6 =$ _____

$9 \times 5 =$ _____

$8 \times 4 =$ _____

$8 \times 6 =$ _____

$5 \times 5 =$ _____

$12 \times 6 =$ _____

$20 \times 4 =$ _____

MINECRAFT FACT: Treasure chests can be buried more than forty blocks down.

Write the answer to each problem. Then cross out the chest with the matching answer below.

4 × 11 = _____   4 × 8 = _____   4 × 10 = _____

5 × 7 = _____   5 × 20 = _____   5 × 9 = _____

6 × 10 = _____   6 × 3 = _____   6 × 6 = _____

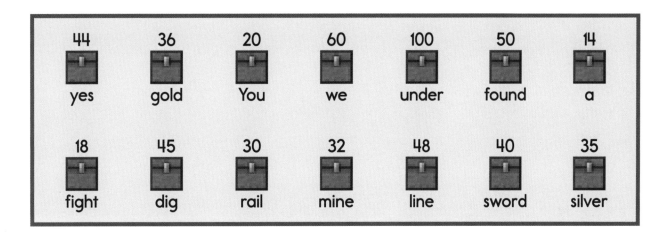

44	36	20	60	100	50	14
yes	gold	You	we	under	found	a

18	45	30	32	48	40	35
fight	dig	rail	mine	line	sword	silver

Copy the words from the chests you didn't cross out. They tell you what happens next.

__ __ __   __ __ __ __ __

__   __ __ __ __ __   __ __ __ __ __ !

You did it! Place your sticker here.

MULTIPLY BY 7, 8, AND 9

You spot an old rail line. Craft a cart so you can speed up your travel.

Solve these **multiplication** problems to craft a minecart.

3 × 7 = _____   9 × 9 = _____

10 × 7 = _____   11 × 8 = _____

2 × 8 = _____   6 × 9 = _____

5 × 8 = _____   20 × 7 = _____

6 × 8 = _____

12 × 9 = _____

MINECRAFT FACT: Minecarts are made with five iron ingots and let you move along tracks in mineshafts.

Connect the minecarts. Draw a line from each cart with a problem to a cart with the correct answer.

When you're finished, copy the letters that did not get crossed into the spaces below for a message.

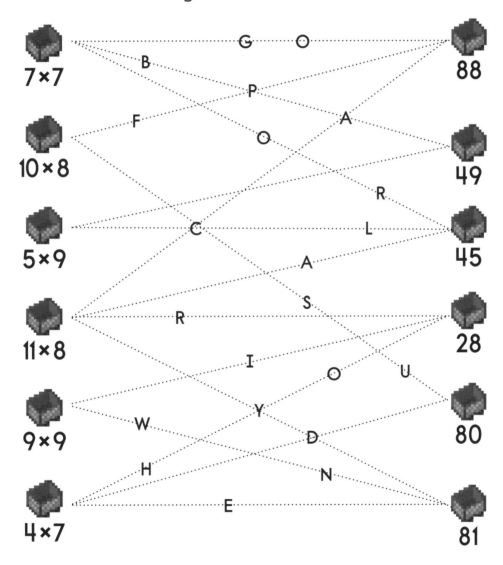

___ ___ ___   ___ ___ ___ ___   ___   ___ ___ ___ ___

You did it! Place your sticker here.

Repair the track, and you'll be ready to roll.

Write the correct answer to fill each gap in the tracks to get from **START** to **END**.

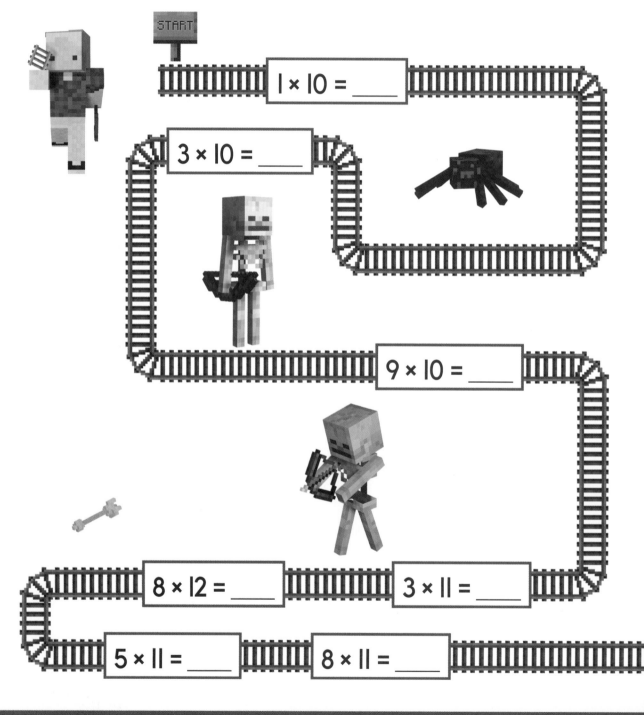

START

1 × 10 = _____

3 × 10 = _____

9 × 10 = _____

8 × 12 = _____   3 × 11 = _____

5 × 11 = _____   8 × 11 = _____

Why did the adventurer quit the battle? *They were a sword loser!*

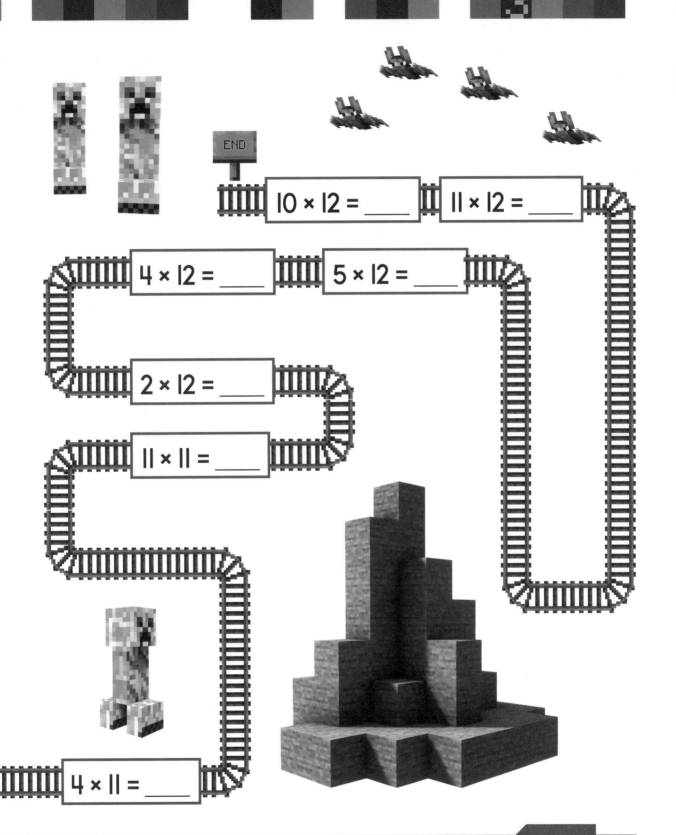

$10 \times 12 = \underline{\hphantom{000}}$

$11 \times 12 = \underline{\hphantom{000}}$

$4 \times 12 = \underline{\hphantom{000}}$

$5 \times 12 = \underline{\hphantom{000}}$

$2 \times 12 = \underline{\hphantom{000}}$

$11 \times 11 = \underline{\hphantom{000}}$

$4 \times 11 = \underline{\hphantom{000}}$

END

You did it! Place your sticker here.

MINECRAFT MISSION

You're ready for a minecart journey. Before you go, try this mission.

This mission sends you on a search *inside* this book. There are items hidden in the top borders of most pages!

Search for pages that have **diamonds** (⬙) hidden at the top. When you find a page with diamonds, multiply the numbers inside them. If the answer is 100, write that page number in the spaces below.

When you've found all three, multiply those numbers and write the answer in the treasure chest.

Then place a sticker and celebrate!

___ **×** ___ **×** ___

=

MINECRAFT

MINE

Great job! You earned a badge! Place your sticker here.

DOWN INTO THE DEEP DARK

You've rolled far into the cave, and you see sculk all around you.

In this adventure, you will...

Follow a sculk vein.

Explore the deep dark.

Evade sculk sensors.

Build wool paths.

Let's get started!

Upon entering the deep dark, you see sculk all around you. Follow the trail of skulk blocks to see where it leads.

Find a path from **START** to **END**. You can only pass through **adjectives** (words that describe something).

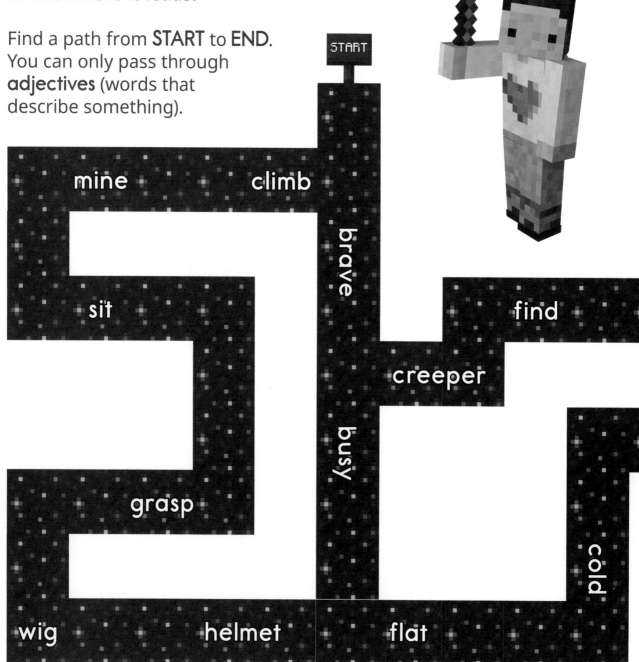

START

mine   climb

brave

find

sit

creeper

busy

grasp

cold

wig   helmet   flat

MINECRAFT FACT: Sculk can only be found in the deep dark.

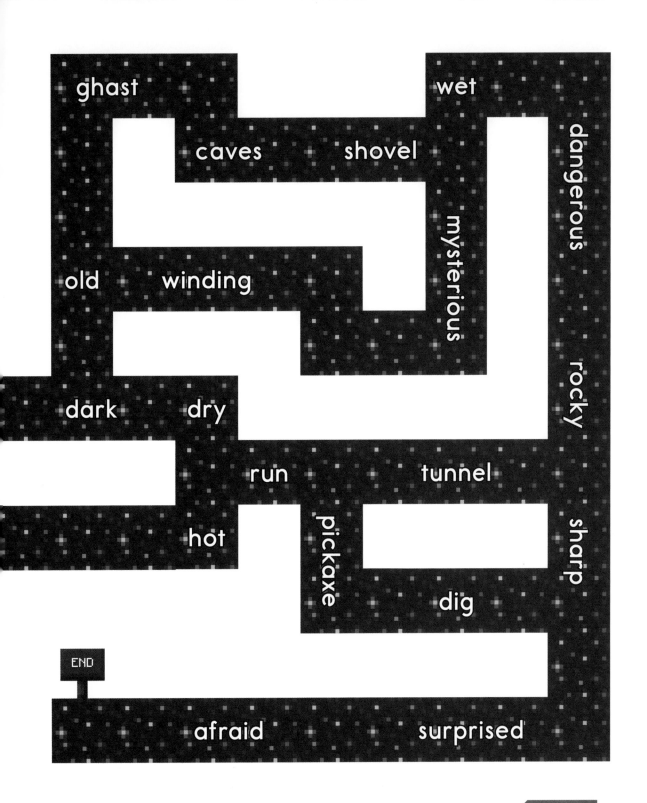

ghast

wet

caves   shovel

dangerous

mysterious

old   winding

rocky

dark   dry

run   tunnel

sharp

hot

pickaxe

dig

END

afraid   surprised

You did it! Place your sticker here.

The vein continues to lead you through the deep dark.

Each set of dots has a number beside it. That is how many lines you should draw to connect the dots. If you connect the right dots, you'll spell three adjectives hidden in the deep dark.

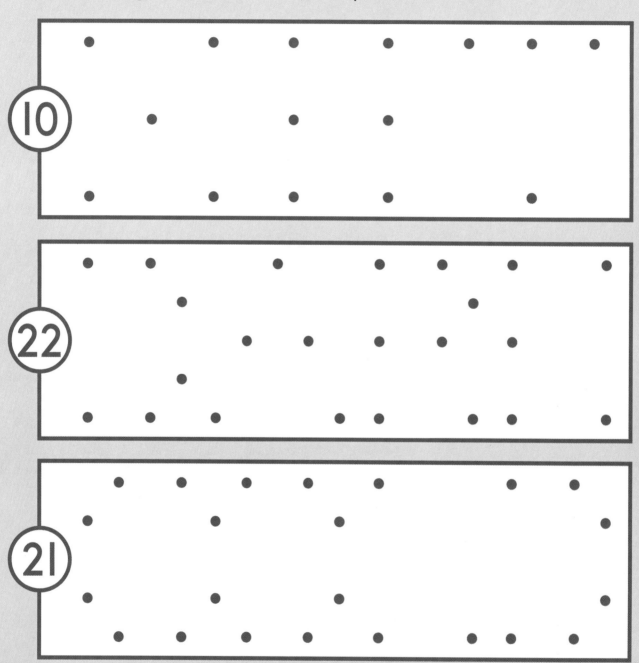

MINECRAFT FACT: Chests in the deep dark's ancient cities contain armor trim smithing templates that you can't find anywhere else.

Draw lines to match each adjective to the correct item in the group.

dark

darker

darkest

small

smaller

smallest

long

longer

longest

least

most

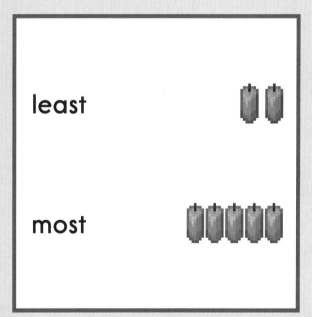

Make sure you don't trip sculk sensors. They could cause a warden to appear.

Circle the **adverb** (word that tells how you do something) under each sensor to sneak past it.

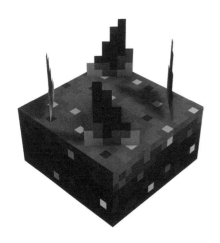 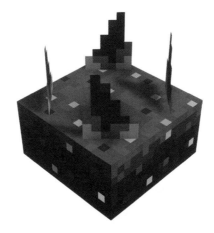 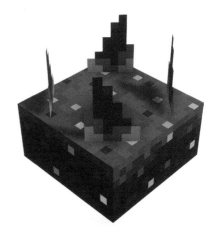

heavy	quiet	slow
deadly	sweet	nicely
heavily	careful	hasty
hairy	hungry	nice
cozy	carefully	costly

MINECRAFT FACT: Sculk sensors detect vibrations and may summon a warden if too much noise is made.

Read each **adjective** and write a matching **adverb.** The first one has been done for you.

sneaky _sneakily_

speedy _____

happy _____

angry _____

hungry _____

Now write two sentences about sneaking past mobs. Try to use as many adjectives and adverbs as you can. You can use words that appear on this page.

_____

_____

_____

Make a wool path. It will silence your footsteps so you don't set off any nearby sculk sensors and summon a warden.

Collect **wool blocks** by matching the given **prefixes** (word beginnings) with each **root word** (the base word).

Use these prefixes:

dis   re   sub   inter

un   de   non   super

_____marine

_____frost

_____visit

_____connect

_____national

_____happy

_____natural

_____stop

How can a warden know which way the wind blows?   *A weather sculk vane!*

Use the wool blocks you collected to complete the path from **START** to **END**. Match each **root word** (the base word) with a **suffix** (word ending) from the word box.

Use these suffixes:

ful	ing	ly	ry	er
ed	able	less	age	ible

START

P R E T E N D ☐ ☐ ☐

A N S W E R ☐ ☐   S L O W ☐ ☐

H E L P ☐ ☐ ☐ ☐   U S E ☐ ☐ ☐

F L E X ☐ ☐ ☐ ☐   B A K E ☐ ☐

T E A C H ☐ ☐   W R E C K ☐ ☐ ☐

END

M E A S U R E ☐ ☐ ☐ ☐

You did it! Place your sticker here.

MINECRAFT MISSION

You're so sneaky! No one heard you on the path. But will they hear you in this mission?

This mission sends you *outside* of this book! Make and play a game with a friend.

Make the game:

- Find crayons and index cards.
- Write each of these letters on separate cards:

A	C	D	E	E	G	H	H	I	M	N	O	R	S	T
A	D	E	E	E	G	H	I	L	N	N	P	R	S	

- Shuffle the cards and deal five to each player.
- Put the rest of the cards in a pile, face down.

How to play:

- On your turn, draw one card.
- If you can spell one of these words with the cards you have, place them down in front of you:

help	the	ender	dragon	is	chasing	me

- If you can't spell one of the seven words, say a letter. If the other player has it, they must give that card to you. (If they have several, they only give you one.)
- Your turn ends when you ask for a letter and the other player doesn't have it. Then it is their turn.
- The first player to spell all seven words and shout, "Help! The Ender Dragon is chasing me!" is the winner.

MINECRAFT

DESCEND

DANGER IN THE DARK

You are traveling through the deep dark when— Uh-oh! You've summoned a warden!

In this adventure, you will...

Escape from the warden.

Make a diamond pickaxe.

Mine obsidian.

Create a Nether portal.

Let's get started!

Be as quiet as you can so you can sneak away from the warden.

Solve these **division** problems to hide.

$8 \div 2 =$ ___ $6 \div 2 =$ ___

$12 \div 3 =$ ___ $6 \div 3 =$ ___

$10 \div 2 =$ ___ $16 \div 2 =$ ___

$18 \div 3 =$ ___ $30 \div 3 =$ ___

$15 \div 3 =$ ___

$9 \div 3 =$ ___

MINECRAFT FACT: A warden can fit in any space that is one block wide and three blocks tall.

Put one number in each empty space to make all the problems true.

$12 \div 2 = \underline{}$

$27 \div \underline{} = 9$

$\underline{} \div 2 = 4$

$21 \div \underline{} = 7$ $30 \div 2 = \underline{}$

$20 \div 2 = \underline{}$ $18 \div \underline{} = 9$

$\underline{} \div 3 = 2$ $3 \div \underline{} = 1$

$18 \div \underline{} = 6$ $\underline{} \div 2 = 2$

You did it! Place your sticker here.

You've evaded the warden. Now is a good time to use the diamonds you brought along. Use them to make a stronger pickaxe.

Solve these **division** problems to gather your materials.

24 ÷ 4 = _____   40 ÷ 4 = _____

20 ÷ 4 = _____   8 ÷ 4 = _____

45 ÷ 5 = _____   15 ÷ 5 = _____

12 ÷ 4 = _____   4 ÷ 4 = _____

25 ÷ 5 = _____

50 ÷ 5 = _____

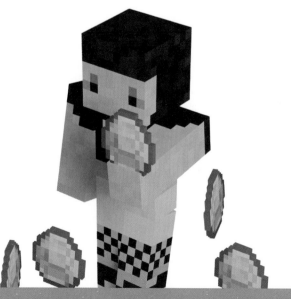

MINECRAFT FACT: *Diamonds can be found in many places, including shipwrecks and abandoned mineshafts.*

Now shade in all the boxes that contain answers to the problems on page 56.

12	12	12	12	2	2	3	3	3	4	4	4	4
12	12	12	2	2	2	3	3	3	10	1	1	4
12	12	11	11	2	2	3	3	3	10	10	1	4
12	11	11	11	8	8	8	8	1	10	10	10	4
11	11	11	11	8	8	8	5	1	1	3	3	3
11	11	11	11	11	8	5	5	5	8	3	3	3
7	7	7	7	7	6	6	5	8	8	3	3	3
7	7	7	7	6	6	6	8	8	8	2	2	2
4	4	4	6	6	6	8	8	8	8	2	2	2
4	4	9	6	6	7	7	7	11	11	11	2	12
4	9	9	9	7	7	7	7	11	11	11	12	12
9	9	9	4	4	4	4	4	11	11	12	12	12
9	9	4	4	4	4	4	4	11	12	12	12	12

You found a lava pool! Pour water on it to make obsidian. Then use your new pickaxe to mine it.

Circle every correct equation. As you find them, circle a block of obsidian at the top of page 59. Then you'll have enough obsidian blocks to create a Nether portal!

$30 \div 6 = 5$

$36 \div 6 = 8$

$36 \div 6 = 6$

$70 \div 7 = 10$

$18 \div 6 = 3$

$54 \div 6 = 9$

$14 \div 7 = 2$

$42 \div 7 = 8$

$21 \div 6 = 4$

$56 \div 7 = 8$

$28 \div 7 = 4$

$50 \div 6 = 10$

MINECRAFT FACT: *You need a diamond or netherite pickaxe to mine obsidian and ancient debris in the Nether.*

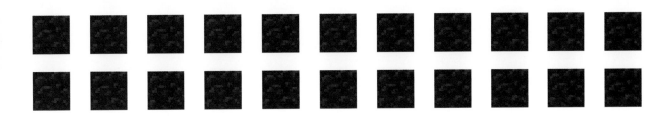

$12 ÷ 6 = 2$

$24 ÷ 6 = 4$

$60 ÷ 7 = 9$

$35 ÷ 7 = 5$

$56 ÷ 6 = 8$

$42 ÷ 6 = 7$

$54 ÷ 7 = 9$

$49 ÷ 6 = 8$

$49 ÷ 7 = 7$

$53 ÷ 6 = 9$

$28 ÷ 6 = 4$

$42 ÷ 7 = 6$

You did it! Place your sticker here.

Loaded with obsidian, you create a Nether portal.

Solve these division problems. Write each answer in the matching shape in the maze. Then find your way from **START** to the Nether portal at **END**. Here's the catch: you can only pass through shapes that have a value of five or less.

$56 \div 8 = \underline{\quad}$ ■

$50 \div 10 = \underline{\quad}$ ●

$8 \div 8 = \underline{\quad}$ ⬣

$90 \div 10 = \underline{\quad}$ ●

$16 \div 8 = \underline{\quad}$ ▲

$70 \div 10 = \underline{\quad}$ ▬

$81 \div 9 = \underline{\quad}$ ★

$24 \div 8 = \underline{\quad}$ ●

$72 \div 9 = \underline{\quad}$ ⬠

$27 \div 9 = \underline{\quad}$ ▮

$36 \div 9 = \underline{\quad}$ ⬟

$64 \div 8 = \underline{\quad}$ ▰

Why did the adventurer start crying? *They found an obsidi-onion!*

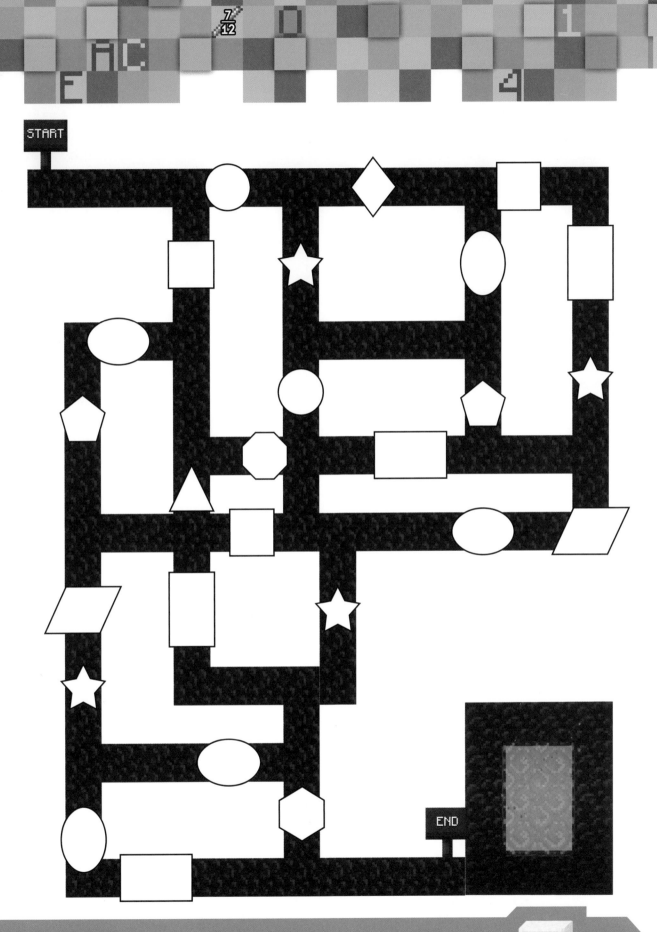

START

END

You did it! Place your sticker here.

You used flint and steel to activate the portal. Before you head in, take this challenge.

This mission sends you on a search *inside* this book. There are items hidden in the top borders of most pages!

Search for pages that have two **pickaxes** (⚒) at the top. Look at the numbers on them.

There are only two pages where you can divide one number by the other and get a value of 3. When you find them, write those page numbers below to form a new problem.

Write the answer in the chest. Then place a sticker to celebrate your success!

_____ ÷ _____ =

Great job! You earned a badge! Place your sticker here.

62

NETHER AGAIN!

You've entered the Nether. There are foes to fight and piglins to barter with.

In this adventure, you will...

Battle ghasts.

Barter with piglins.

Fight blazes.

Head home with your loot.

Let's get started!

Wouldn't you know it? As soon as you set foot in the Nether, ghasts attack! Evade their fireballs.

Draw a straight line to connect each pair of **synonyms** (words that mean the same thing). When you're finished, copy the leftover letters into the spaces below.

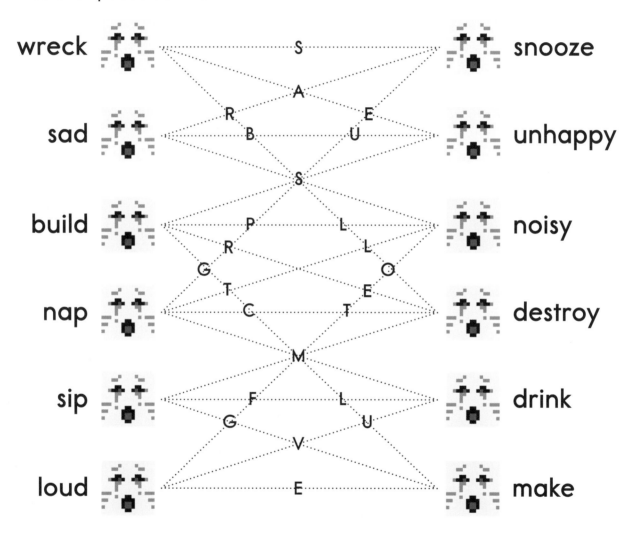

What's a synonym for **rescue**?

___ ___ ___ ___

MINECRAFT FACT: Piglins will barter with you if have gold ingots.

Defend against each fireball with a **synonym**. Write one synonym under each shield.

expert

_____

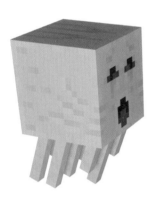

silent

_____

near

_____

Ahh, piglins. If you're lucky, they'll swap Ender pearls for your gold ingots.

Draw lines to connect each pair of **antonyms** (words that mean the opposite).

hot	dry
straight	cold
wet	hard
light	curvy
short	tall
easy	thin
fast	slow
thick	dark

MINECRAFT FACT: Piglins will always spawn within bastion remnants.

Write an **antonym** under each piglin.

under

_____

bored

_____

difficult

_____

hidden

_____

dangerous

_____

sleeping

_____

You arrive at a fortress when blazes suddenly appear! If you defeat them, they may drop a blaze rod that you can pick up.

Read the word above each blaze. Below each one is two **homophones** (words that sound the same but have different meanings). Circle the homophone that has the same meaning as each blaze's word to defeat it.

noticed

seen   scene

earned

won   one

correct

write   right

pause

wait   weight

uncovered

bare   bear

also

too   two

MINECRAFT FACT: Nether fortresses are structures in the Nether. They have blaze spawners and rooms connected by long bridges.

Cross out every pair of matching **homophones**. Write the leftover words in the spaces below.

bear   two   through   steel
   blaze   rods

right   are   fuel
   meddle   write

one   won   bare
   and   you

can   craft   threw   with
   steal   wait

medal   weight   them   too

__ __ __ __ __   __ __ __ __

__ __ __   __ __ __ __   __ __ __

__ __ __   __ __ __   __ __ __ __ __

__ __ __ __   __ __ __ __

HOMONYMS

Head home with your new pearls and rods. Things are looking good. Once you've left the Nether, you can prepare for a final battle.

Each word in the box below is a **homonym** (a word spelled the same but with a different meaning) and matches two separate definitions on the path out of the Nether.

Find a path from **START** to **END**. When you reach a definition, identify the homonym, then jump to the word's second definition. But be careful! Some jumps will lead to dead ends or closed loops.

Use these words:

bark	mine
bat	saw
bear	store
light	watch

a large, furry animal

a small, winged animal

a small clock worn on the wrist

START

to look closely at something

a supply or stock

What do Wither skeletons wear to look fancy? Blazers!

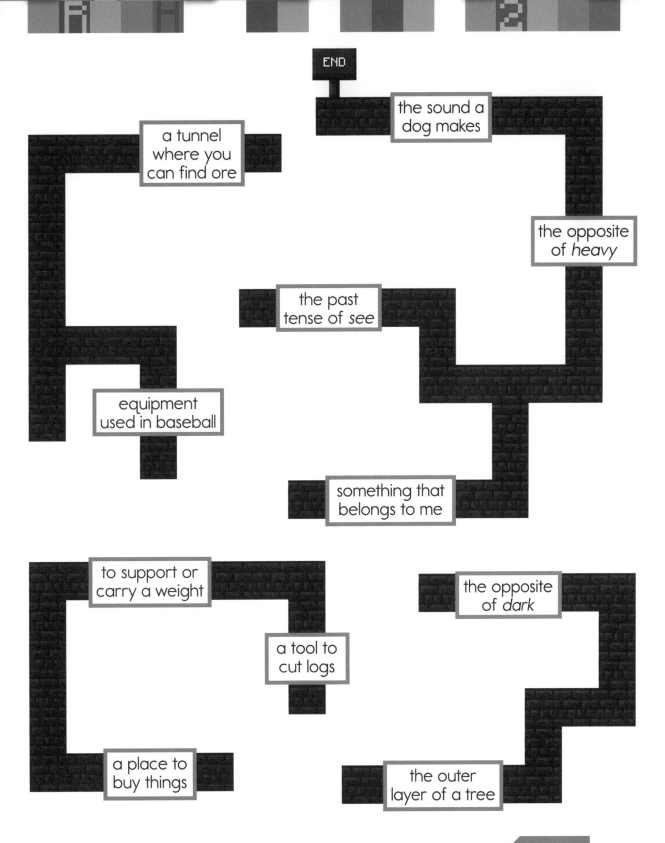

END

the sound a
dog makes

a tunnel
where you
can find ore

the opposite
of *heavy*

the past
tense of *see*

equipment
used in baseball

something that
belongs to me

to support or
carry a weight

the opposite
of *dark*

a tool to
cut logs

a place to
buy things

the outer
layer of a tree

You did it! Place your sticker here.

You've left the Nether. Prepare for a final Minecraft battle with a challenge that sends you around the real world.

This mission sends you *outside* of this book! Go on a quest to find things that are **homonyms** and **homophones** in real life.

Search your house for words on boxes, book covers, and other places that are either homonyms or homophones. Remember **bark** and **bark**? **Steel** and **steal**?

Write down the word pairs you find. If you can find two pairs, you're pretty good. If you can find four pairs, you're a Minecraft mission champ!

When you think you've found all that you can, celebrate with a sticker on this page!

_____   _____

_____   _____

_____   _____

_____   _____

MINECRAFT

FIGHT

Great job! You earned a badge! Place your sticker here.

FIND THE PORTAL!

You're getting close to the ultimate battle. Open the End portal!

In this adventure, you will....

Craft eyes of Ender.

Locate a stronghold.

Dig deep.

Activate an End portal.

Let's get started!

Craft blaze rods into blaze powder. Then craft the blaze powder with Ender pearls to create eyes of Ender.

Write the **fraction** made by the colored part of each group. The first one has been done for you.

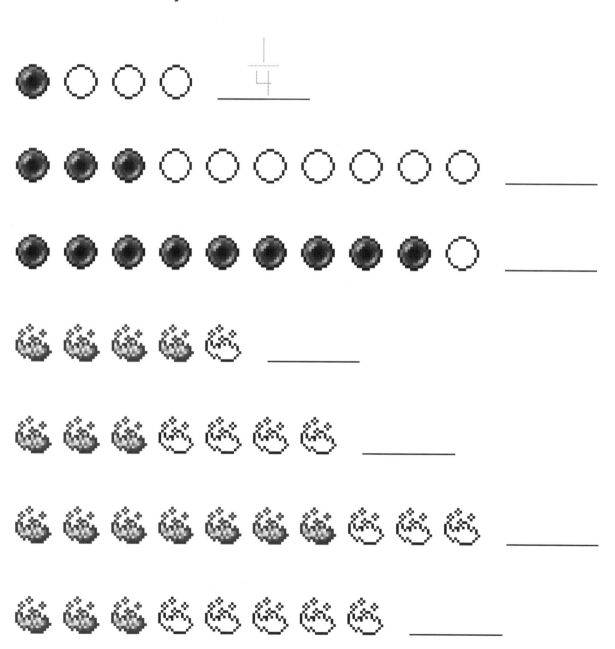

$\dfrac{1}{4}$

MINECRAFT FACT: Blaze powder can fuel brewing stands, brew potions of Strength, and make eyes of Ender.

74

Color the correct number in each group to represent the **fraction** that is shown. The first one has been done for you.

$\frac{1}{2}$ ● ● ● ● ○ ○ ○ ○

$\frac{7}{10}$ ○ ○ ○ ○ ○ ○ ○ ○ ○ ○

$\frac{2}{3}$ ○ ○ ○ ○ ○ ○ ○ ○ ○

$\frac{1}{5}$ ○ ○ ○ ○ ○

$\frac{1}{2}$

$\frac{1}{4}$

$\frac{6}{6}$ 🐷 🐷 🐷 🐷 🐷 🐷

$\frac{1}{5}$ 🐷 🐷 🐷 🐷 🐷 🐷 🐷 🐷 🐷 🐷

Grab your gear and toss your eye of Ender. It will lead you to a stronghold.

Color in the amount represented by each **fraction** to move down the path from **START** to **END**. Keep going until you reach the spot where your eye of Ender has landed.

MINECRAFT FACT: Strongholds are usually located very deep underground.

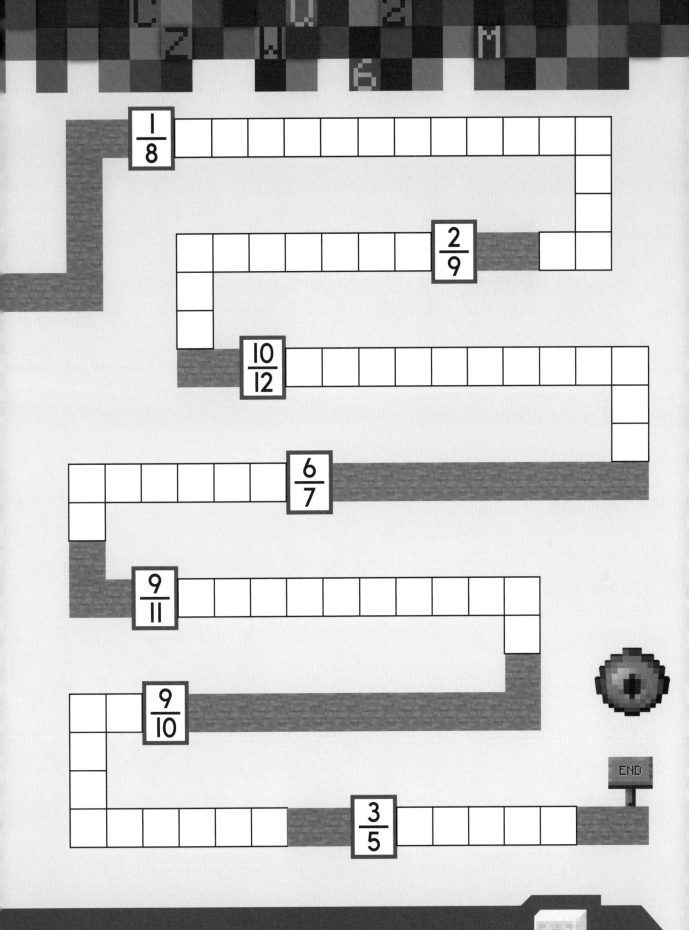

$\dfrac{1}{8}$

$\dfrac{2}{9}$

$\dfrac{10}{12}$

$\dfrac{6}{7}$

$\dfrac{9}{11}$

$\dfrac{9}{10}$

$\dfrac{3}{5}$

END

You did it! Place your sticker here.

Your eye of Ender has disappeared into the ground! Dig to reach the stronghold.

Write a **fraction** under each pit to show how much of the hole you still have to dig to reach the stronghold. Then write the **decimal** that has the same value. The first one has been done for you.

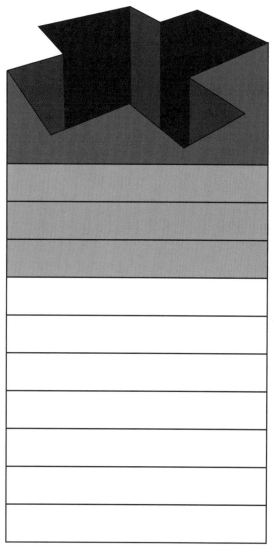

$$\frac{3}{10} \qquad 0.3$$

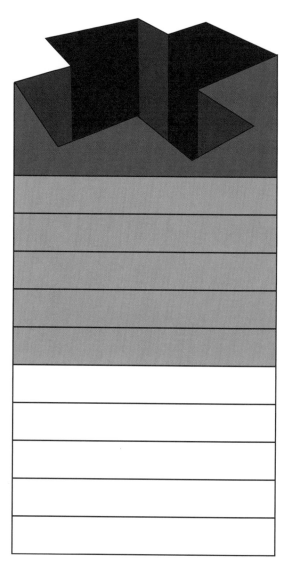

_____ _____

MINECRAFT FACT: Strongholds can contain different types of rooms. It may take some searching to find the portal room.

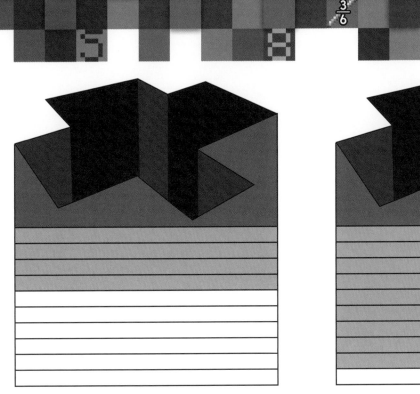

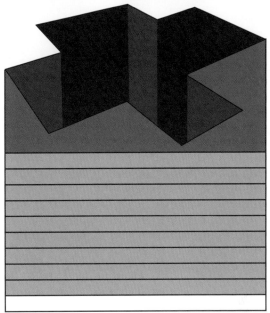

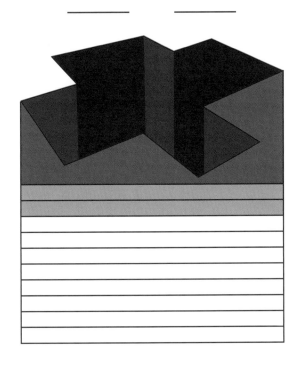

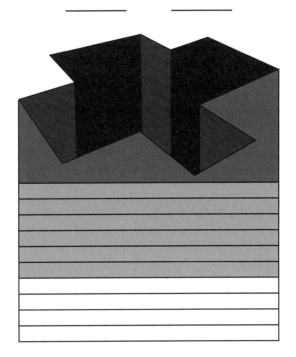

The stronghold has an End portal. Place the eyes of Ender into the portal frame to activate it.

Find a path from **START** to **END** through the maze of fractions and decimals. You can only pass through if the value shown is equal to **0.5** or less.

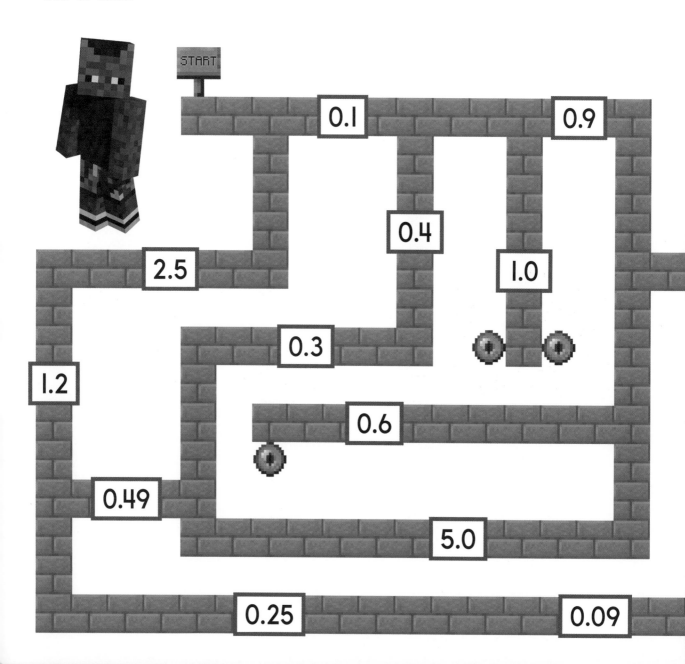

How did the cat make eyes of Ender?   *It used Ender purrs!*

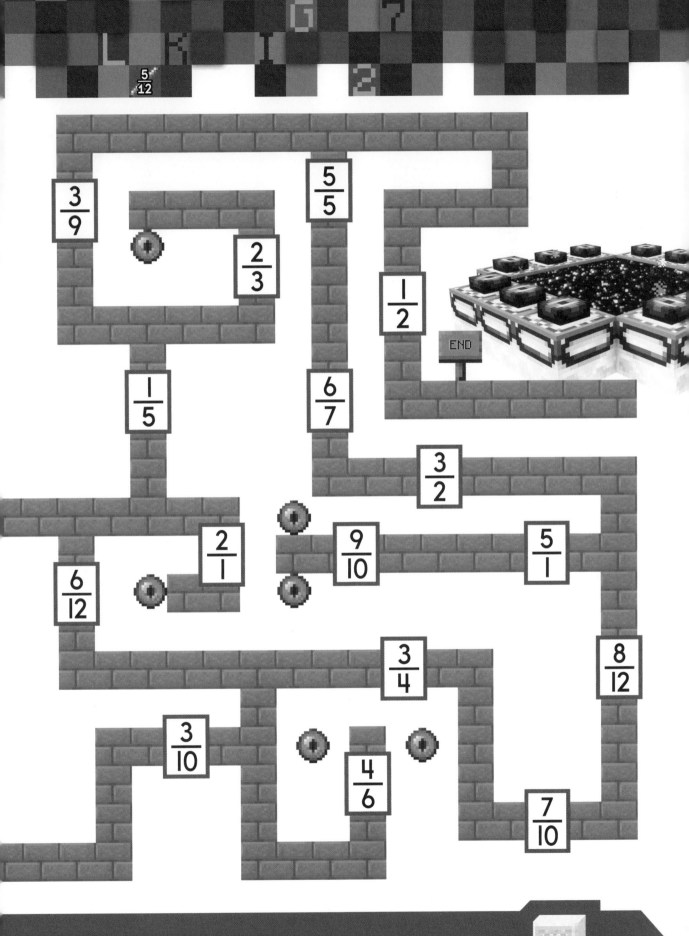

$\frac{5}{12}$

$\frac{3}{9}$

$\frac{5}{5}$

$\frac{2}{3}$

$\frac{1}{2}$

END

$\frac{1}{5}$

$\frac{6}{7}$

$\frac{3}{2}$

$\frac{6}{12}$

$\frac{2}{1}$

$\frac{9}{10}$

$\frac{5}{1}$

$\frac{3}{4}$

$\frac{8}{12}$

$\frac{3}{10}$

$\frac{4}{6}$

$\frac{7}{10}$

You did it! Place your sticker here.

The only thing standing between you and the End portal...is this mission.

This mission sends you on a search *inside* this book. There are items hidden in the top borders of most pages!

Search for **blaze rods** (✎). Each has a fraction on it.

There are many to find, but only three have the same value as $\frac{1}{2}$. Write those fractions in the spaces below.

_____ _____ _____

Write the three that have the same value as $\frac{1}{3}$.

_____ _____ _____

Write the three that have the same value as **1**.

_____ _____ _____

Great job! You earned a badge! Place your sticker here.

MINECRAFT

BATTLE

FINAL SHOWDOWN

Entering a new dimension, you see something circling in the sky.

In this adventure, you will...

Encounter the Ender Dragon.

Break End crystals.

Dodge attacks.

Defeat the flying beast!

Let's get started!

What's that in the sky? It's the dreaded Ender Dragon!

Unscramble these words and write them in the spaces on page 85. When you are done, read the whole sentence. It will tell you why an Ender Dragon is so tough to defeat.

tI   si

rahd   ot

etaefd   het

ednEr   gaonrD

aseebcu   ti

ash   laienhg

ewpro

MINECRAFT FACT: The Ender Dragon is the only one of its kind in Minecraft.

You spot crystals atop obsidian pillars. Fire arrows to break them.

The word search on page 87 is filled with words that go up, down, across, backward, and diagonally. Once you've circled all the words, write the leftover letters in the spaces below. They'll spell what happened to the dragon.

Find these words:					
answer	between	eat	from	rough	steal
because	bunch	enough	new	route	sure
begin	decide	few	own	saw	

___ ___   ___ ___ ___ ___

___ ___ ___ ___ ___ ___ ___

___ ___ ___ ___ !

MINECRAFT FACT: The End crystals at the tops of the obsidian pillars regenerate the Ender Dragon's health.

```
I  A  N  S  W  E  R  E  B
T  E  L  L  A  E  T  S  E
D  N  H  C  N  U  B  U  G
E  O  O  S  O  T  H  A  I
C  U  E  R  U  S  S  C  N
I  G  E  A  L  I  A  E  N
D  H  G  U  O  R  W  B  W
E  F  R  O  M  N  G  P  O
B  E  T  W  E  E  N  O  W
E  W  R  T  A  E  N  E  W
```

With the dragon's healing power gone, you stand a fighting chance. Go, go, go!

Read each statement about the battle and answer the questions.

I spotted the dragon high in the sky. Suddenly it dove to fight me.

Which direction did the dragon go?

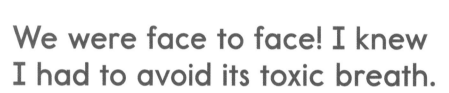

_____

We were face to face! I knew I had to avoid its toxic breath.

What's a word that describes the dragon's breath?

_____

I thought about all the gear I had with me. I grabbed the long, sharp blade by its small handle.

What did you grab?

_____

MINECRAFT FACT: When using its breath attack, the Ender Dragon spews purple clouds that deal damage.

I was beginning to think that I couldn't defeat the dragon.

Were you sure you would win?

_____

I swung a dozen times. Then I did it two more times. It was exhausting!

Did you swing the weapon more than twenty times?

_____

My sword connected! With the dragon now damaged, things were finally starting to go my way.

What did the sword touch?

_____

The dragon's health is almost at zero. Now it's up to you to decide how you'll finish this battle!

Use your imagination and number the pictures in the order you think they might happen.

Then write a sentence or two under each box and tell your own story of how you defeated the dragon!

_____

_____

_____

_____

_____

_____

Why did the creature scuff up the floor? *It was dragon!*

_____

_____

_____

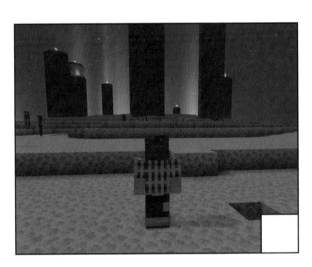

_____

_____

_____

You did it! Place your sticker here.

MINECRAFT MISSION

You defeated the Ender Dragon. You're a hero in Minecraft...and beyond!

You've discovered so many things within these pages! Now try one last mission *outside* this book and search for things in the real world.

Below is a list of things to find on an ultimate scavenger hunt. Search in places like your kitchen or living room. Look inside books or on boxes and cans. You can search outside, too.

If you can find four of these things...not bad. Find all six things on this list, and you're a Minecraft Mission Superstar!

Super Scavenger Hunt:

- Something with at least two different **fractions** on it

- Something with a **two-digit number** that you can divide by five

- Something with two numbers on it that equal 24 when you multiply them together

- Something with at least three **adjectives** on it

- Something with at least two **adverbs** on it

- Something that has a **singular** and **plural** version of the same word on it

Great job! You earned a badge! Place your sticker here.

ANSWERS

Pages 4–5

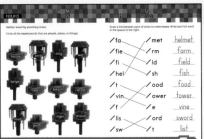

Pages 6–7

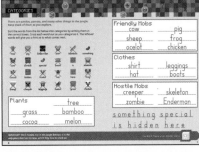

Pages 8–9

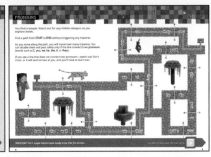

Pages 10–11

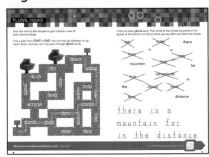

Pages 14–15

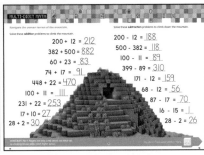

Pages 16–17

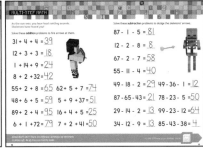

Pages 18–19

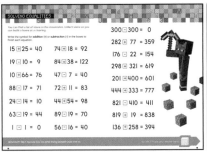

Pages 20–21

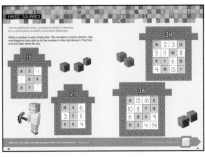

Page 22

Pages 24–25

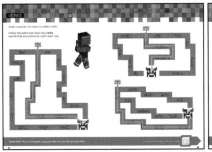

Pages 26–27

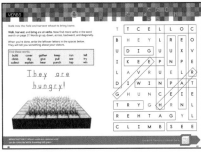

Pages 28–29

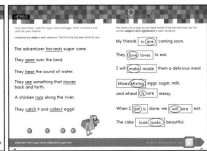

Pages 30–31

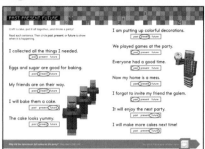

PAST, PRESENT, FUTURE

Craft a cake, put it all together... and throw a party!

Read each sentence. Then circle *past*, *present*, or *future* to show when it is happening.

I collected all the things I needed.
past present future

Eggs and sugar are good for baking.
past present future

My friends are on their way.
past present future

I will bake them a cake.
past present future

The cake looks yummy.
past present future

I am putting up colorful decorations.
past present future

We played games at the party.
past present future

Everyone had a good time.
past present future

Now my home is a mess.
past present future

I forgot to invite my friend the golem.
past present future

It will enjoy the next party.
past present future

I will make more cakes next time!
past present future

Pages 34–35

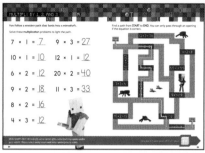

MULTIPLY BY 1, 2, AND 3

You follow a wooden path that leads into a mineshaft.

Solve these multiplication problems to light the path.

7 × 1 = 7   9 × 3 = 27
10 × 1 = 10   12 × 1 = 12
6 × 2 = 12   20 × 2 = 40
9 × 2 = 18   11 × 3 = 33
8 × 2 = 16
4 × 3 = 12

Find a path from START to END. You can only pass through an opening if the equation is correct.

Pages 36–37

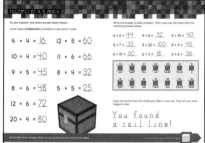

MULTIPLY BY 4, 5, AND 6

As you explore, you come across many chests.

Solve these multiplication problems to see what's inside.

4 × 4 = 16   12 × 5 = 60
10 × 4 = 40   11 × 6 = 66
9 × 5 = 45   8 × 4 = 32
8 × 6 = 48   5 × 5 = 25
12 × 6 = 72
20 × 4 = 80

Write the answer to each problem. Then cross out the chest with the matching answer below.

4 × 11 = 44   4 × 8 = 32   4 × 10 = 40
5 × 7 = 35   5 × 20 = 100   5 × 9 = 45
6 × 10 = 60   6 × 3 = 18   6 × 6 = 36

Copy the words from the chests you didn't cross out. They tell you what happens next.

You found
a rail line!

Pages 38–39

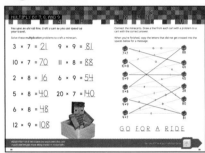

MULTIPLY BY 7, 8, AND 9

You spot an old rail line. Craft a cart so you can speed up your travel.

Solve these multiplication problems to craft a minecart.

3 × 7 = 21   9 × 9 = 81
10 × 7 = 70   11 × 8 = 88
2 × 8 = 16   6 × 9 = 54
5 × 8 = 40   20 × 7 = 140
6 × 8 = 48
12 × 9 = 108

Connect the minecarts. Draw a line from each cart with a problem to a cart with the correct answer.

When you're finished, copy the letters that did not get crossed into the spaces below for a message.

GO FOR A RIDE

Pages 40–41

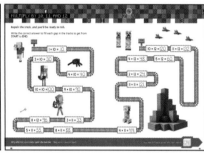

MULTIPLY BY 10, 11, AND 12

Repair the track, and you'll be ready to roll.

Write the correct answer to fill each gap in the tracks to get from START to END.

1 × 10 = 10
3 × 10 = 30   4 × 12 = 48   5 × 12 = 60
4 × 10 = 40   2 × 12 = 24
10 × 10 = 100   9 × 10 = 90   3 × 11 = 33
                 6 × 11 = 66
8 × 12 = 96   3 × 11 = 33
5 × 11 = 55   8 × 11 = 88   4 × 11 = 44

Page 42

MINECRAFT MISSION

You're ready for a minecart journey. Before you go, try this mission.

This mission sends you on a search inside this book. There are items hidden in the top borders of most pages!

Search for pages that have diamonds (◇) hidden at the top. When you find a page with diamonds, multiply the numbers inside them. If the answer is 100, write that page number in the spaces below.

When you've found all three, multiply those numbers and write the answer in the treasure chest.

Then place a sticker and celebrate!

6 × 7 × 20

= 840

Pages 44–45

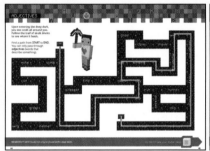

ADJECTIVES

Upon entering the deep dark, you see scrub all around you. Follow the trail of skulk blocks to see where it leads.

Find a path from START to END. You can only pass through adjectives (words that describe something).

Pages 46–47

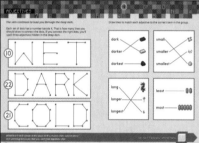

ADJECTIVES

The veins continue to lead you through the deep dark.

Each set of dots has a number beside it. That is how many lines you should draw to connect the dots. If you connect the right dots, you'll spell three adjectives hidden in the deep dark.

10 WET
22 DARK
21 COLD

Draw lines to match each adjective to the correct item in the group.

dark   small
darker   smaller
darkest   smallest

long   least
longer   most
longest

Pages 48–49

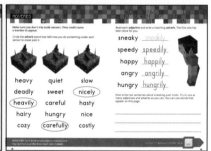

ADVERBS

Make sure you don't trip aside mobs. They could come a warden to appear.

Circle the adverb (word that tells how you do something) under each sensor to sneak past it.

heavy   quiet   slow
deadly   sweet   nicely
heavily careful hasty
hairy   hungry   nice
cozy   carefully costly

Read each adjective and write a matching adverb. The first one has been done for you.

sneaky   sneakily
speedy   speedily
happy   happily
angry   angrily
hungry   hungrily

Now write two sentences about sneaking past mobs. Try to use as many adjectives and adverbs as you can. You can use words that appear on this page.

Pages 50–51

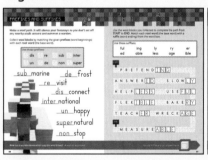

PREFIXES AND SUFFIXES

Make a small path. It will silence your footsteps so you don't set off any nearby skulk sensors and summon a warden.

Collect skulk blocks by matching the given prefixes (word beginnings) with each root word (the base word).

dis re   sub inter
un   de   non super

sub marine   de frost
re visit
dis connect
inter national
un happy
super natural
non stop

Use the word blocks you collected to complete the path from START to END. Match each root word (the base word) with a suffix (word ending) from the word box.

Use these suffixes:
ful ing ly   ry   er
ed   able less age ible

P R E T E N D I N G
A N S W E R S L O W L Y
H E L P L E S S U S E F U L
F L E X I B L E B A K E R Y
T E A C H E R W R E C K A G E
M E A S U R E A B L E

Pages 54–55

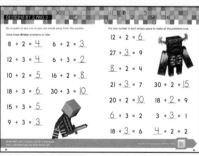

DIVIDING BY 2 AND 3

Be as quiet as you can so you can sneak away from the warden.

Solve these division problems to hide.

8 ÷ 2 = 4   6 ÷ 2 = 3
12 ÷ 3 = 4   6 ÷ 3 = 2
10 ÷ 2 = 5   16 ÷ 2 = 8
18 ÷ 3 = 6   30 ÷ 3 = 10
20 ÷ 2 = 10   18 ÷ 3 = 6
18 ÷ 3 = 6   4 ÷ 2 = 2

Put one number in each empty space to make all the problems true.

12 ÷ 2 = 6
27 ÷ 3 = 9
8 ÷ 2 = 4
21 ÷ 3 = 7   30 ÷ 2 = 15
20 ÷ 2 = 10   18 ÷ 2 = 9
6 ÷ 3 = 2   3 ÷ 3 = 1

Pages 56–57

DIVIDING BY 4 AND 5

You've reached the warden. Point to a good item to see the diamonds you brought along. Use them to make a stronger pickaxe.

Solve these division problems to gather your materials.

24 ÷ 4 = 6   40 ÷ 4 = 10
20 ÷ 4 = 5   8 ÷ 4 = 2
45 ÷ 5 = 9   15 ÷ 5 = 3
12 ÷ 4 = 3   4 ÷ 4 = 1
25 ÷ 5 = 5
50 ÷ 5 = 10

Now shade in all the boxes that contain answers to the problems on page 56.

Pages 58–59

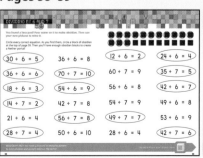

DIVIDING BY 6 AND 7

You found a lava pool! Pose nearer so it can make division. Then use your new pickaxe to mine it.

Circle every correct answer. As you find them, circle a block of obsidian at the top of page 59. Then you'll have enough obsidian blocks to create a Nether portal!

30 ÷ 6 = 5   36 ÷ 6 = 6   12 ÷ 6 = 2   24 ÷ 6 = 4
36 ÷ 6 = 6   70 ÷ 7 = 10   60 ÷ 7 = 8   35 ÷ 7 = 5
18 ÷ 6 = 3   54 ÷ 6 = 9   56 ÷ 6 = 8   42 ÷ 6 = 7
14 ÷ 7 = 2   42 ÷ 7 = 8   54 ÷ 7 = 9   49 ÷ 6 = 9
21 ÷ 6 = 4   56 ÷ 7 = 8   49 ÷ 7 = 7   53 ÷ 6 = 9
28 ÷ 7 = 4   50 ÷ 6 = 10   28 ÷ 6 = 4   42 ÷ 7 = 6

Pages 60–61

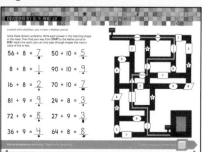

DIVIDING BY 8, 9, AND 10

Loaded with obsidian, you create a Nether portal.

Solve these division problems. Write each answer in the matching shape in the maze. Then find your way from START to END through shapes that have a value of five or less.

56 ÷ 8 = 7   50 ÷ 10 = 5
56 ÷ 8 = 7   90 ÷ 10 = 9
16 ÷ 8 = 2   70 ÷ 10 = 7
81 ÷ 9 = 9   24 ÷ 8 = 3
72 ÷ 9 = 8   27 ÷ 9 = 3
36 ÷ 9 = 4   64 ÷ 8 = 8

Page 62

MINECRAFT MISSION

You travel Nest, and need to activate this portal. Before you head in, take this challenge.

This mission sends you on a search inside this book. There are items hidden in the top borders of most pages!

Search for pages that have two pickaxes (⛏) at the top. Look at the numbers on them.

There are only four pages where you can divide one number by the other and get a value of 5. Write those page numbers below to form a new problem.

Write the answer in the chest. Then place a sticker to celebrate your success!

66 ÷ 11 = 6

94

Page 64

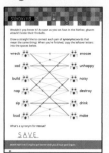

SYNONYMS

Synonym matching exercise

wreck, sad, build, nap, tip, loud

snooze, unhappy, noisy, destroy, drink, make

What's a synonym for **rescue**?

SAVE

Page 66

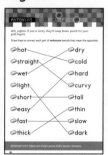

ANTONYMS

- hot — dry
- straight — cold
- wet — hard
- light — curvy
- short — tall
- easy — thin
- fast — slow
- thick — dark

Pages 68-69

HOMOPHONES

noticed   earned   correct

pause   uncovered   also

blaze rods
are fuel and
you can craft
with them

Pages 70-71

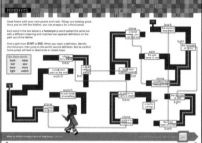

HOMONYMS

Pages 74-75

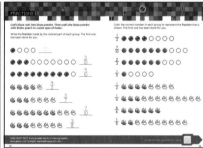

FRACTIONS

Pages 76-77

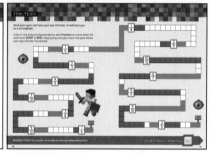

FRACTIONS

Pages 78-79

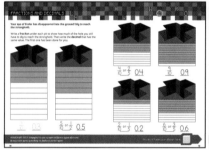

FRACTIONS AND DECIMALS

Pages 80-81

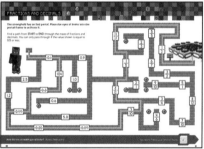

FRACTIONS AND DECIMALS

Page 82

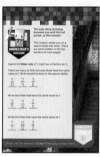

Page 85

It is hard
to defeat the
Ender Dragon
because it
has healing
power.

Pages 86-87

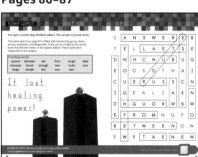

SIGHT WORDS

It lost
healing
power!

Pages 88-89

READING COMPREHENSION

I spotted the dragon high in the sky. Suddenly it dove to fight me. Which direction did the dragon go?

down

We were face to face! I knew I had to avoid its toxic breath. What's a word that describes the dragon's breath?

toxic

I thought about all the gear I had with me. I grabbed the long, sharp blade by its small handle. What did you grab?

a sword

I was beginning to think that I couldn't defeat the dragon. Were you sure you would win?

no

I swung a dozen times. Then I did it two more times. It was exhausting! Did you swing the weapon more than twenty times?

no

My sword connected! With the dragon now damaged, things were finally starting to go my way. What did the sword touch?

the dragon

MINECRAFT ACHIEVEMENT

GRADE E

Let it be known
throughout the End:

_____
YOUR NAME

has completed an
adventure filled with
MINECRAFT MISSIONS!